Healing
Your
Insecurities

Healing
Your
Insecurities

by
Roy H. Hicks, D.D.

HARRISON HOUSE
Tulsa, Oklahoma

Unless otherwise indicated,
all Scripture quotations are taken from
the *King James Version* of the Bible.

7th Printing
Over 45,000 in Print

Healing Your Insecurities
ISBN 0-89274-249-6
Copyright © 1982 by Roy H. Hicks, D.D.
1100 Glendale Boulevard
Los Angeles, California 90026

Published by Harrison House, Inc.
P. O. Box 35035
Tulsa, Oklahoma 74153

Contents

Preface

Recently my good friend, Dr. Roy Hicks, asked me to read the manuscript of a new book he had written. Having received pleasure and spiritual uplift from several of his previous books, I responded to the request with considerable enthusiasm.

After reading one chapter, I felt certain this would be one of the most helpful and challenging works to come from the pen of Dr. Hicks.

In his writings Dr. Hicks always hits upon a subject that is both unique and eminently practical. This present work shares this originality and may turn out to be the most practical of all his books.

Healing Your Insecurities concerns a problem with which a great many of us have wrestled. I know the problem well and wish I had read such a book fifty years ago.

The trauma of insecurity manifests itself in many symptoms. Unfortunately, we struggle long with the symptoms without even suspecting their cause or origin. By spending much time in the Word of God, we may conquer the symptoms one by one, but how much more readily and thoroughly we could overcome them if we had clear insight into the cause of them.

The Bible has wonderful healing for insecurity. But the symptoms are such that we seldom recognize insecurity as the cause. We try to deal with the symptoms instead of getting at the cause.

When God heals the fountain, the bitter waters will turn to sweet. This very frank discussion of insecurity, if read with an open mind, should help many Christians to find the biblical remedy for the emotional immaturity displayed by others. Dr. Hicks deals with the problems faced by those who are argumentative, competitive, thin-skinned to criticism, boastful, domineering, maladjusted as parents or spouses, or overindulgent in food or drink.

After putting a finger on the cause of these problems, Dr. Hicks leads the reader to scriptural resources for healing and gives examples of the kind of prayer that brings victory.

Healing Your Insecurities should prove to be very helpful for discussion in youth groups where its insights may head off early in life the effects of childhood insecurities. It should be recommended reading for parents. It helps explain some of the frictions in marital relations and provides guidance for parents who want to avoid the development of insecurity in their children.

Pastors will find the insights provided by this book to be very useful in their ministry of counseling, enabling them to get at the source of problems for which their troubled church members seek counsel.

May God bless this volume with the wide circulation it deserves.

Nathaniel M. Van Cleave, D.D.

Introduction

This is a simple, short, direct book — a result of my years of experience in dealing with many Christian people. The majority of these, I came to realize, were beset with problems caused by deep-rooted insecurity, either their own or those of the people with whom they were having the difficulty.

Titles of some of the ensuing chapters are: "Competition," Who Is To Blame?" "Inability To Trust," "Obesity," and "Criticism." Do any of these chapter headings speak to you?

Jesus Christ our Lord is the epitome of a secure person. Though He was divine, He lived on earth as a human being, facing all the limitations of the physical body as we do. Because He now lives within us, as believers, we can allow *His* security to become *our* security, overcoming *our insecurity.*

One of the great hindering factors facing counselors is the difficulty in getting insecure people to face their insecurity. Until they do, very little help will be forthcoming. The Apostle Paul faced his insecurity in 1 Corinthians 13:11. He wrote:

When I was a child, I spake as a child, I understood as a child, I thought as a child: but when I became a man, I put away childish things.

I had counted myself to be a very secure Christian, not realizing how many lifelong habits and reactions were a result of insecurity. Writing this book has been a great help in causing me to face these and do something about them. I hope reading it will do the same thing for you.

1
Security vs. Insecurity

Therefore if any man be in Christ, he is a new creature; old things are passed away; behold, all things are become new.

2 Corinthians 5:17

The memory of the just is blessed.

Proverbs 10:7

"The memory of the righteous continues a blessing."

Berkeley Version

For he hath made him to be sin for us, who knew no sin; that we might be made the righteousness of God in him.

2 Corinthians 5:21

The psychologists teach that most all adults have either a little boy or a little girl living inside them. If this is true, then most human behavioral problems could easily stem from scars left deeply imprinted in people's minds.

If your childhood memories and experiences continue to have a bearing on your psyche, you do indeed need to endeavor to become a new creature in Christ Jesus. As long as the old things, especially experiences, have direct influence on your daily life, you cannot, as a believer, have full benefit of your new life in Christ Jesus.

If you first face the possibility that the small child you were is yet being dealt with, you can easily understand why so many people have to continually deal with their insecurities.

As a child, you charged, then retreated; you tried to come on boldly, courageously, determined. That strong expression of your emerging will was met with the equally strong parental "no"—or perhaps even with the back of a hand! Then you no doubt sought another way to satisfy your growing curiosity; you tried to find fulfillment of your unalienable rights. You longed for some kind of recognition in a very strong, adult-dominated world. Or, you may have been babied, coddled, and spoiled. If your every whim was granted, you ended with even greater scars because you were not then learning obedience.

Those painful and harsh childhood experiences are buried somewhere deep within you. You either seek to become a new creature in Christ totally, or you continue to give way to the little child.

Have you heard of an adult pouting because he did not get his own way, even going for weeks without speaking to someone?

Have you witnessed the violent temper—things thrown, vitriolic words angrily spoken—that is later regretted?

Grown men fighting, even killing, to save face or to prove a very minor point?

No doubt the adult world is much closer to childishness than anyone would care to acknowledge. As someone has said, "You either parent the child or give in to him."

If what a Christian receives with his salvation is immediate perfection, including complete security, you may expect to be continually surrounded by an adult church—a church made up of people completely free from insecurity. This would mean that there would be no more church quarrels and splits, no more marital strife and divorces. A perfect love would be shown by all and to all.

Since this isn't the case, you can assume that your insecurities must be dealt with, and your new life of security in Christ your Lord must be cultivated continuously and be coveted above all else.

Maturity and security are strong words; insecurity and childishness are fearful words. Security and trust are words of peace. Fear and unbelief are words of torment. Security and generosity are the opposite of insecurity and selfishness.

As God our Father looks down upon us, He sees us as believers 100 percent pure and holy, because he views us through the mighty sacrifice of His Son, Jesus, on the cross. In the eyes of God, a believer is as much a completed saint the day he is saved as he will ever be, whether he lives one hour or a hundred years.

We cannot, by works, improve on our standing with God. Jesus our Lord not only died for us, shedding His precious blood for our sins, He also gave to us, as a free gift, His own perfect righteousness.

There are no great laws we must fulfill to get to heaven. There are no great sacrifices to make. The laws were all fulfilled for us by our Lord. The complete sacrifice was made. All anyone needs to do is believe the Gospel story of our Lord and receive Him as personal Savior. That's all!

What then are we to contribute? We get to become partners with Jesus in God's Kingdom. We are permitted to share that wonderful new life with the world around us. We get to pray, give, and love. For these things we will be rewarded after we get to heaven and hear Him say, "Well done, thou good and faithful servant."

There are other things we are privileged to do. We get to crucify the old nature and put it under. We get to cultivate good fruit — to watch the old man die and the new man being renewed day by day.

If we fail to recognize our weakness and our insecurities, they will remain very much a part of our lives. We will then remain as a baby Christian, immature and dominated by the carnal flesh. Childhood behavioral habits will try to surface and rob us of a glowing testimony and maturing life.

If Christian fruit were automatic, all would have an equal portion. If Christian maturity were natural, it would be seen equally by all. If godly temperament were the Christian norm, we could forget about church fights and splits. There would be none.

One of the damaging things that can happen when great truths are being reemphasized is that those truths can become substitutes for the Lord Jesus as our security.

Submission is a biblical truth. Its new emphasis was needed, but some have allowed those to whom they were submitting to take the place of their Lord.

Faith's confession is a great truth, much needed by the Church, but we must not prostitute this biblical truth by making it merely a way to ''get things from God.'' God wants us to claim what belongs to us. His provision for us is healing and prosperity. But if having these things becomes your security, it is misplaced security! The Lord Jesus, our wonderful Savior Who purchased these things for us, must always be our only security.

Security, as it relates to everyday living, can only surface and become part of us as our insecurity is recognized and dealt with. James 5:16 states it so well: *Confess your faults one to another, and pray one for another, that ye may be healed.* We do need that confessing, recognizing those inherited weaknesses that war against us as believers. Then the wonderful security of our Lord Jesus, the Perfect One Who lives in us, will emerge; and we will walk in newness of life as mature and secure saints of God.

A Prayer

Dear Father, there is nothing I desire more in this life than for others to see Your beauty in me. I desire to become a big person. I don't want the weakness of the flesh to continually surface and be seen in me.

As I become acquainted with and acknowledge my insecurities that bind and hinder my desire to be like You, help me to overcome them. Help me to allow that wonderful security I have in You to become my life-style.

I don't want the little child that I once was to dominate me. I want You to live big in me. I confess my faults and weakness to You now. I believe with my heart and say with my mouth: Old things are passing away and all things are becoming new.

In Jesus' name,
Amen.

2
Competition

You can be sure that by connecting insecurity with competition, you will cause a few competitive eyebrows to be raised. Competition has become the norm for the American way of life. Up to 75 percent of passing-the-time-of-day conversation usually is centered around the daily sports page or local sporting events. In some families, the members are competing somewhere every day or night in the week.

In no way do I intend to raise the pen against enjoyable competition that is usually centered around good fellowship—the playing of parlor games, electronic or mechanical. These are generally beneficial, even to raising healthy-minded children.

What I do intend to point out is the wrong that is caused and promoted by the form of competition fostered in the average school, college, and home. Believe it or not, it's spilling over into church life.

What are 100,000 fans doing as they sit on a cold, wintry, rainy day, watching their favorite team play? As they sit in the stands, what do they see on the field? Do they see a big lineman trying to put the quarterback out of the game, or a fleet halfback scoring a touchdown? No, they see themselves the hero. Their security and identity is vicariously transferred to another who is strong, fast, and effective—something that they fancy they might have done or become. It wasn't to be, so they have settled for fantasizing by watching others, and they will pay whatever it costs to do so.

Did God intend for man to strive to win at any cost, to beat someone into submission, to cheat and buy out the referee? Or did He create us to strive only to be excellent, to excel only to better ourselves to endeavor to amount to something?

The Bible speaks to us about God creating and that all He created is very good. (Gen. 1.) God gave us excellent minds and bodies. With that mind and body, He gave us good desires to work hard to better ourselves. We were created to become excellent, to excel in all we do, but not at the expense of another human being; not to humiliate and shame another, even to the point of causing physical harm and/or emotional trauma.

When the games we play for pleasure and pastime are carried a little further, they become war games: generals strategically placing their armies to win, not always for survival.

They think, "What and where can we conquer next?" One notorious leader wept because there were no more worlds to conquer.

Where does this kind of competition come from? From Satan. He said:

I will ascend into heaven, I will exalt my throne above the stars of God: I will sit also upon the mount of the congregation, in the sides of the north: I will ascend above the heights of the clouds; I will be like the most High.

Isaiah 14:13,14

This spirit of competition—the spirit of pride that destroys; the need to be king at any cost and lord it over another human being, eventually even God—is from the regions below, and should be recognized for what it is and be dealt with.

This spirit of satanic competition with pride as its basis has spilled over into the Church, even into church sports and, therefore, does not accomplish the original intent: fellowship and fun. The same spirit that was taught in high school, college, and professional sports—the spirit of winning at any cost—goes so far in some churches that they actually recruit certain people to attend their church, just so they can be on the team.

Is the Church so insecure in Christ that it has to resort to winning at any cost to achieve the kind of security it thinks it needs in order to be accepted in the community? Is not our Lord's salvation and hope all the security we need? While it is true that some churches seem to be able to participate with a Christian spirit, this is not the norm.

What about the Christian home — the competition between husband and wife? They play the one-upmanship game: husband putting down wife, wife putting down husband, even in front of their children.

One will not allow the other to excel in a gift. Sometimes the wife knows history or English better than the husband. She is the one qualified to help the children with their homework, especially in the area of her expertise. The husband may know about arithmetic. He can shine there!

Do we allow this to flow normally? No. Usually we wait until one makes a slight error, then the spouse pounces on it with a put down. Is it because we don't love each other? Not usually. It is out of deep childhood insecurity that has crept over into adulthood. We are so insecure that we seize on every opportunity to make ourselves look good at the expense of others.

Is your insecurity showing in this area? Here's a good test to give yourself to check and see. The next time someone begins to tell a joke that you have already heard, are you secure enough to allow him the spotlight for a few moments or do you speak up and say, "I have already heard it"? Or, after he is through, do you say, "That's not the way I heard it"? Is it so important to your security that you must rob that person of a little joy in relating an incident or telling a story so you can have a little attention?

Here is another test to give yourself: Do you allow your spouse or your children to tell something that relates to a family vacation or happening without constantly interrupting? Are you secure enough to allow them to miss some minor points without correcting them publicly?

I used to do this until I discovered I had been doing it from childhood insecurity that was carried over into adulthood.

Children reared in an atmosphere of one-upmanship and of putting each other down are being taught insecurity. This kind of competition is wrong. They can be taught correctly. They can learn how to excel and better themselves by learning how secure they can become as believers in Christ, rather than being taught how to have false security by winning the wrong way.

Children should be taught that they have security, even when they lose. They should be taught how to accept themselves under all situations, whether winning or losing. They need to know that God loves them just as much and that you as parents also appreciate and love them, regardless of whether or not they make the team, whether they win or lose.

Jesus our Lord seemed to be a loser. Wasn't He on the cross for all to see and ridicule? He seemed to be a failure: even His disciples thought so. He lost His life, laid it down, so all of us could be made winners in His finished work. Even in death, we are winners.

Teach this to your children. Learn to overcome the insecurities passed on to you through the horrors of being a loser during some competitive event. Your child may have been defeated because he lost to someone more skilled. Don't tease or put him down or remind him of your accomplishments. Make him to know where the true security is: in Christ, our Lord.

Believers in the Lord Jesus have all the security they need to see them through this life. We are winners. All we need to do is read the last page and our hands are raised in triumph! We are not *going to be* winners; we are winners *already*, seated with Christ in the heavenlies. We need to hear ourselves speaking like we are already on the other side.

A Prayer

Dear Heavenly Father, in Jesus' name, help me not to rely on how the whistle blows in this life, not to depend on the score for my happiness. Help me know that the game of life is already settled.

The enemy that was out to destroy me is already defeated. I didn't have to beat him. He was defeated at the cross. I am a winner through Christ Jesus my Lord.

Amen.

3
Who Is To Blame?

This "security robber" raises its ugly head very early in the Bible. This weakness in mankind originated with the first man, Adam.

When the voice of God challenged the first man and asked if he had eaten of the forbidden fruit, we witness the finger of accusation promptly pointing to the woman, Eve. Then we hear our first *Who is to blame?* A slogan is born: "It had to be somebody else. I can't be the guilty one."

Adam said, *The woman whom thou gavest to be with me, she gave me of the tree, and I did eat* (Gen. 3:12).

Is this tendency to blame someone else a trait of mankind, a human characteristic; or is it the first result of coming face to face with a weakness in Adam that we all must eventually come to grips with at some time in our life?

Did Adam actually think that by placing the blame on Eve he would appear more righteous in the sight of God? In this kind of emotional response, and without time to think, did he somehow seek to conceal his own weakness and failure in the transgression? Certainly he was not, in love and compassion, thinking of Eve in her plight.

Whether this weakness is Satan-inspired or man-inherited, we must deal with it and come face to face with this robber of our security in Christ. This we must do if we are to come into the full inheritance and maturity of our Lord's security for our soul.

This insecurity is with us from our earliest recollection. Some children have heard one of their parents say, ''If

I had married someone else, we wouldn't be so poor,'' or ''I could have had a better job if my parents had put me through college.''

You might have heard an adult blame his or her boss for the failure to get ahead. A person of great success is often described as having been ''born with a gold spoon in his mouth'' and ''really lucky!'' There is an attitude of envy: ''*I* wasn't born with a gold spoon in *my* mouth!'' Sometimes failure is blamed on poor education, lack of opportunity, even on ethnic background.

When we became old enough to participate in sporting events, someone else was always picked out to be blamed for the loss of the game: ''The pitcher never threw me a good ball,'' ''The umpire made bad calls,'' ''It was a fluke; that fielder was out of position when he caught my fly ball—it was headed for the stands," "Any team can win when the ref is on its side!"

A friend of ours was struck by a car that was going the wrong way on a freeway. At the scene of the accident, the driver of the errant car was irritated with my friend and said petulantly, "Everyone else got out of my way! Why didn't you?"

The long list of reasons why we fail can easily follow us into our relationship with the Lord. I have heard many working pastors say, "If I only had more time to study and pray, I know my church would grow." Laymen have said the same thing in relation to their own personal growth: "If I sat under that pastor's ministry, I would really grow." A pastor might say, "I have never been appointed to a good church. I only get the burnt-out ones."

The obvious answer to this weakness of criticism, inherited from our parents and contemporaries, is to recognize that it stems from deep-seated insecurities, so deep that often they are buried in the subconscious mind. By recognizing these insecurities and dealing with them, the beauty of Christ-related security can then be loosed in us and begin to develop.

While it is true that the thought of *Who is to blame?* does have some merit at times, it is also true that constantly confessing and acknowledging it will do nothing towards erasing or changing the past.

Forgetting those things which are behind . . . .

Philippians 3:13

In Christ Jesus our Lord lies our new sense of security. Not only are we to forget the past by not referring to it, we are to constantly refer to the present and to the fact that we are new creatures in Christ.

Who is to blame? can become much greater than just a security robber. Its ugly tentacles can reach into the depth of a person's soul and cause him even to blame God. Deep subconscious (I surely hope no one would consciously do it) resentment of God Himself can result from an uncontrolled resentment of others.

"Did not God, our Creator, make all things? Then why did He make me so ugly when others are beautiful? Why me, Lord?"

"Why am I so large and awkward; others so petite and agile?"

"Why was I born of poor parents?"

"Why was I born in poverty?"

This sort of questioning, if unchecked, can cause us even to resent our Creator. On the other hand, history relates how many of the handicapped went on to great fame and fortune because they stopped feeling sorry for themselves.

Who Is To Blame?

Why blame someone else? You are what you are, so go on to become the greatest mature Christian that ever lived. You can do it. Don't blame anyone for your failure to achieve; just rejoice that your name is written in heaven (Luke 10:20) and see what great things the security of Christ's righteousness can do in you.

Confessions

Thank You, Lord. You said, so I can also say, I am more than a conqueror.

I can do all things in Christ, no matter what the circumstances are.

Greater is He that is in me than he that is in the world.

My security is not in what I think I am, but in who You say I am.

I will never again blame anyone else.

I will arise and meet every new day with joy and faith, forgetting yesterday.

I will leave all failures out of my vocabulary.

I will become all that You have promised I can become.

A Prayer

Dear Father, in Jesus' name, I ask Your forgiveness to cover any hidden resentment I might possibly have against You. I know that You created us perfect in the beginning. Because of the fall of our Adamic parents, that beautiful creation has been marred. I am a product of that sin.

Because I am a new creation in You, please help me to allow that life to flow out of me. Please allow Your security to become my security. I will no longer blame anyone. I will endeavor to become all that You originally intended—a beautiful example of Your redeeming love.

Amen.

4
Inability To Trust

Many of us know people who cannot delegate. Their desks are always piled high and they are likely to talk about how busy they are. This inability to be a trusting person, even carrying over into the inability to delegate, has at its roots deep insecurity.

Our Lord Jesus, even at age twelve, was surprised that His parents could not trust Him to be about His Father's business. Is it possible that Jesus was such a secure person that He assumed His parents were as secure as He was? Like most of us, they came from such an unstable hereditary environment that it was difficult for them to be the trusting people their son expected them to be.

Mary and Joseph lived in an environment of negatives. Probably every day the conversation was mixed with uncertainties and hearsay. Rumor and horror-filled happenings were the topics of the day's chatter. The future was always clouded with gloomy predictions.

Inasmuch as people don't really change, they probably talked constantly about the scarcity of food and its unbelievable cost; constantly about the political situations and, of course, how leadership could never be trusted.

It probably sounded much like the twentieth-century environment in which we were raised. The kind of society we were born into does not produce secure adults. Even after we receive the Lord Jesus and His sacrificial death, and know that our names are written in The Book, we remain basically insecure. Our destination changes, some of our habits change, but seldom does our old nature become entirely a new one.

Most of our inability to trust in God comes from an insecure, unstable past. Our subconscious minds have been so permeated by the ravages of sin-blighted humanism that it is difficult to become God-trusting people.

Many Christians grow up hearing more about the failure of prayer than about its success. We hear more about God punishing man than about His being good to them. We hear far more unanswered questions about His nature than we do clear-cut explanations of His faithfulness.

After we become Christians, we fight a continuous battle with doubt, fear, and unbelief.

Like so many others, I have had to battle a childhood fear that as soon as all was going well and things were getting easier, look out—that's just the time I could be hit by an avalanche of trouble. "If the farmers had a bumper crop this year, they are sure to have three years of drought." "If someone seems happily married, just wait awhile and their troubles will begin. The honeymoon won't last!"

The many insecurities of a godless society become deeply entrenched in our minds. These insecurities when brought over into our Christian faith inhibit us greatly, dogging our path and harassing us relentlessly.

Many pastors and leaders have great difficulty in delegating authority and responsibility because they have never faced the underlying reasons. They need to confess this weakness and be healed from these insecurities by constantly acknowledging God's security that is in them by salvation.

Our Lord Jesus sets good examples for us to follow. He delegated authority and trusted that things would be carried out: the fetching of the colt to ride during the triumphant entry, the securing of a room for the Last Supper, the handling of finances by another, the feeding of the multitude.

When He returned to heaven, He delegated to us the authority to use the keys of the Kingdom here on earth.

And I will give unto thee the keys of the kingdom of heaven: and whatsoever thou shalt bind (stop) *on earth shall be bound in heaven: and whatsoever thou shalt loose* (allow) *on earth shalt be loosed in heaven.*
Matthew 16:19

Not only does our insecurity interfere with our simple faith in God and in prayer, it even interferes with our trusting each other. Our backbiting, our gossipy nature, our running each other down, come from childhood insecurities.

By reading the Psalms carefully, you will notice how often our fears and insecurities are mentioned first, then the call to trust in the Lord.

Israel was extremely insecure after having been in Egypt for over 400 years. Even after God sent Moses, delivered them, supplied them with all they needed, and even caused their shoes to last 40 years, they couldn't trust God to take them into the Promised Land.

Many times Christians can relate past answers to prayer and tell of their glories. But today they are experiencing difficulty due, I am sure, to the unfaced insecurities of childhood hang-ups.

We, as the Psalmist, must *closet ourselves in the sanctuary* to take care of the emotional pressure we sense as we live in a God-hating world. (Read Ps. 73.)

There seem to be two types of Christians, one by far in the majority. The verse most of these people quote is Psalm 56:3, *What time I am afraid, I will trust in thee.* A very good verse. But notice this person is saying, "When fear comes, I will trust God." It is almost as if he is saying, "I know fear is on its way; when it comes, I will trust Him."

The other Christian, the one in the minority, is quoted in the same chapter, verse 11: *In God have I put my trust: I will not be afraid what man can do unto me.* This Christian has a relationship with his Lord that supersedes fear. He is always ready for anything that can happen. This relationship with the Lord seems to be the obvious answer to the insecurity dilemma.

This relationship with the Lord is a daily walk with Him, a trusting fellowship. The insecurities of the past and the insecurities constantly surrounding us will not automatically fade away. They must be faced with a constant confession of who we are in Christ, what He has done for us, and what He has prepared for us.

Instead of confessing what we can't do, let us say boldly, *I can do all things through Christ which strengtheneth me* (Phil. 4:13).

Instead of confessing our weakness, let us remind ourselves that the Word teaches us to say, *Let the weak say, I am strong* (Joel 3:10).

Instead of confessing our sickness and infirmities, let us confess, . . . *with his stripes we are healed* (Is. 53:5).

No longer should we talk about the weak society surrounding us, but of the heavenly host surrounding us.

''I refuse to let my mouth violate my believing heart by uttering anything that defeats the finished work of my Lord Jesus on the cross for me.

''My insecurities fade away as I realize my security in Christ. I trust Him, so I can now be more trusting with others. I can delegate others to help me, and even let them get all the credit, for I am a secure person in Christ.''

Is it possible that most divorces have as their chief cause deep insecurity, the inability to trust each other?

Marriage does not change personalities. It does not erase childhood patterns and, in most cases, does not erase insecurity. In fact, if the insecurities are there, it may even magnify them.

I would strongly urge all married couples to take time to discuss with each other any problems they feel have followed them from a very insecure childhood. Sometimes it is financial; it could be sexual, even loneliness. Face them, get them out in the open, and begin to allow the security of the Lord to surface in your lives, thus in your home. Become trusting spouses.

Confession/Prayer

I will face any insecurities that hinder me from trusting others. If I cannot delegate, there must be a reason. Lord, help me to face up to this weakness.

As I grow in my ability to trust You, Lord, I should grow in my ability to trust others.

If I am not growing in my ability to trust others, to delegate, even to allow others to receive credit, then it is possible, Lord, that I am not trusting You as I should. My confession is, I will overcome all my insecurities and become a trusting soul by Your help.

Amen.

5
Obesity

Then was Jesus led up of the Spirit into the wilderness to be tempted of the devil. And when he had fasted forty days and forty nights, he was afterward an hungered. And when the tempter came to him, he said, If thou be the Son of God, command that these stones be made bread.

But he (Jesus) answered and said, It is written, Man shall not live by bread alone, but by every word (rhema) that proceedeth out of the mouth of God.

Matthew 4:1-4

The account of Satan's temptation of Jesus, prior to His earthly ministry, is not only packed full of spiritual applications, but is filled with practical, everyday helps and aids, even to curbing the appetite for food.

Jesus had not yet entered into His deliverance and teaching ministry. He had to prove that He could overcome the physical and spiritual temptations that, given time, will assail all of us.

How could our Lord help His fellow man be a strong witness to the love and power of His heavenly Father, with full inward knowledge and peace? He could not until He Himself had experienced personal victory over all of Satan's efforts, especially the temptation to the flesh.

Let us deal with the insecurity question as it relates to the problem of obesity, gluttony, and overindulgence.

Someone recently wrote about the shock he received when returning from several months abroad. It seemed that every American was terribly overweight, especially in comparison to the people of other countries. Yes, despite all we hear about dieting, exercise, jogging, bicycling, and health spas, Americans still eat far too much and it usually shows.

If Christians had a built-in security just because they were Christians, it is probable that every believer would be naturally trim and slim. If true, one of our appeals to the sinner who was overindulgent would be, "Get saved and lose weight." To know this isn't true, all you need to do is look around the next time you go to church. You will know that church members have the same weakness as the world. You can't hide it.

Do we have to prove a connection between obesity and insecurity? I don't believe so. It is a common belief shared by all psychologists.

As I was talking with a Christian who has had a lifetime battle with excessive overweight, he related how it all began when he was four years old. His parents began to have trouble with their marriage; so instead of taking a teddy bear to bed, he would take food. When things were calm at home, he had less trouble; when things were bad, he ate more.

Many people with a weight problem can easily trace its beginning to some kind of traumatic troubles, either with family members or with society in general.

Food is a natural tantalizing pacifier. There is just something about satisfying the taste buds that gives temporary security. This exercise in futility reminds me of the angel in Revelation saying of ''the little book,'' . . . *it shall make thy belly bitter, but it shall be in thy mouth sweet as honey* (Rev. 10:9). In other words, ''You're gonna pay for that sweet tooth!''

As we read in Matthew 4:2, Jesus had fasted forty days and forty nights.

Notice again how carefully the Scriptures are written. The phrase "day and night" is used because the Jews practiced a short fast. After He had fasted and denied His body food for so long, the hunger pains must have been uncontrollably fierce. It was at this precise time that Satan came and tempted Him with food, then connected the temptation with security: *If thou be the Son of God . . . .*

Satan's temptation was, "If you don't eat, you'll die." He was suggesting to Jesus that getting food into His body was His security, rather than trusting His Father's Word.

By living in a human body Jesus had learned enough to know that it must have food or it will die. But He also knew His heavenly Father. His security was in God, not in food or anything else earthly. For Him, it would be better to die of starvation than to rebel against His Father and obey Satan.

Thank God, it is recorded for us how Jesus gained victory over the temptation of the flesh and food. He said, *Get thee behind me, Satan.* He satisfied His tongue with speech, rather than the taste of food. Our wonderful Lord Jesus quoted Scripture, *Man shall not live by bread alone.* In other words, man cannot survive by bread only; he must also live by the Word of God.

By the quoting of this Word, you can learn a great psychological and spiritual truth: If you are not keeping the precarious balance between your bodily and spiritual appetites, you are out of balance and your obesity is telling everyone the truth—the whole truth!

You might answer, "I have tried everything: prayer, diet, exercise. Nothing works." But the Word of God works. It worked for Jesus and it will work for you!

The secret here lies in the tongue—that little culprit with the big taste buds, that little instrument set on fire of hell. The more you eat, the more your taste buds will want. Try satisfying them by the instruction found in Proverbs 16:24:

Pleasant words are as an honeycomb, sweet to the soul, and health to the bones.

Speaking the Word of God will not only satisfy your craving taste buds, but will also feed your inner man; and the happier he is, the less trouble you'll have with the outer man.

If obesity is your problem, then rich, caloric food must become your enemy. For instance, when others are indulging in some sweet delicacy, you need to say to yourself (out loud when you're sure you won't offend someone), ''Pie, ice cream, sweet roll, candy . . . you are my enemy. You are out to destroy me. You are my temptation in the wilderness. You tempt my taste buds. You're out to send me to an early grave, to shorten my life.''

Someone once said, "Inside every fat person is a thin one, clamoring to get out."

The Word of God tells us that if we destroy our bodies, which are temples of God, God will destroy us. Our bodies are not saved. They are just along for the ride, and protesting our every attempt to be spiritual! (The last thing to be redeemed is the body.) Nevertheless, we are commanded to keep our bodies under control.

The Apostle Paul deeply respected the power of his body as he spoke about it in 1 Corinthians 9:27:

But I keep under my body, and bring it into subjection: lest that by any means, when I have preached to others I myself should be a castaway (disqualified).

The Hebrew children knew about eating the right kind of food so that they could survive in a very unfriendly and hostile environment. Our twentieth-century, luxurious style of living can be very contrary to scriptural teaching. The more you recognize your security in Christ your Lord, the less insecure you will feel in this present-day environment. You don't need to turn rocks into bread. You first learn to feed your heart with God's Word by reading it and speaking it.

The sweet bread of God's security (God's Son was that bread come down out of heaven) will satisfy the taste buds: *O taste and see that the Lord is good* (Ps. 34:8). Then the earthly food (Jesus did eat and you have to also) will not dominate you. In your newfound security in Christ, you will always be on top, victorious over all things.

A Prayer

Dear Lord Jesus, forgive me for giving in to the temptations of my appetite. Forgive me for attempting to turn everything into bread. Help me to know that because I am Your child, I am secure.

Food will no longer be my security. I will not turn to it when I feel depressed, rejected, or lonely; I will turn to You. I will taste and see and know that You, the Lord, are always best for me.

By Your help, Lord, I will know that certain kinds of food are not good for me. I will resist it. I will call it what it is—my enemy—and will say, "Enemy, get behind me." I shall not live by bread/sweets alone, but by every word that comes from God's mouth to my mouth.

I am secure because You, the Bread of heaven, are my security.

Amen.

6
Carnal Brain vs. Mind of Christ

*For to be carnally minded is death; but to
be spiritually minded is life and peace.*
                                    Romans 8:6

"For the mind of the flesh is death;
but the mind of the Spirit is life and
peace."
                        American Standard Version

*Because the carnal mind is enmity
against God . . . .*
                                    Romans 8:7

"This is so because the fleshly mind
hates God."
                                                Beck

One of the chief areas, from which
spring deep insecurities that follow us

into our Christian life, is our brain which remains carnal. We call it the carnal mind. It will be this brain that decays with the rest of our body when we die. It will decay with all its carnal memories of profanity and unclean thoughts, with all its memories of hurt and pain, never to be remembered again.

All of us have the same battles with the carnal mind. Some battle evil thoughts; some battle pride. With many it is habitual worrying. The carnal mind is there; it doesn't just go away because we receive forgiveness for our past sins. We are admonished by the Scriptures not to give in to that mind, but to strive to be spiritually minded. All of us know what a constant battle it takes.

Philippians 2:5 teaches, *Let this mind be in you, which was also in Christ Jesus.* The mind of our Lord Jesus was set on one thing: to obey His Father and suffer the death of the cross. He could have had some difficulty with His fleshly mind, which I call the brain, as He wrestled with it in the Garden of Gethsemane. The mind of the flesh, or brain, did not want to suffer the pains of the cross; but the mind of Christ won as He said, ''Not My will, but Thine be done.''

Here is an apt description of the brain, the fleshly mind, that wants to worry instead of trust: It will recall evil jokes at the most inauspicious occasions and gladly retain all memories of sin and of pain. It is that with which we struggle when the beauty of the opposite sex challenges our desire to be spiritual.

The Apostle Paul wrote to the Galatians about living the crucified life:

I am crucified with Christ: nevertheless I live; yet not I, but Christ liveth in me: and the life which I now live in the flesh I live by

*the faith of the Son of God, who loved me,
and gave himself for me.*

Galatians 2:20

Since we as Christians do not
believe, as some religions do, in
physically abusing and mutilating the
flesh, it must then be in the mind that
our battle takes place.

What is that part of our mind which
would refuse such a sacrifice as our
wonderful Lord provided? We attend
church and enjoy Bible studies. We
gather with the saints to worship. But
there is one part which refuses to
cooperate and refuses to receive: the
part that was in rebellion for so many
years, the part that enjoys the thoughts
of sin and its pleasure. I call it the brain,
the carnal brain—the part of our soulish
nature that refuses to die, refuses to
bend or bow. As the little child put it
when the teacher made him stand in the
corner, ''I may be standing on the
outside, but I'm sitting on the inside.''

Could this be the reason so many sincere believers fall by the wayside and return to sin as a pig to the mud? Could this be Satan's playground?

Notice the Apostle begins Galatians 2:20 with a beautiful fact: *I was there when Jesus died. I died with Him, and He now lives in me.*

What part of me does He live in? If He is living in my brain, my carnal thoughts, then it is terribly embarrassing. If He is living somewhere else in me, good! I need to know that. It makes me feel terribly insecure to think He is dwelling in my brain, thinking my thoughts. If Jesus is not in my brain, then it is going to be easier to overcome my hang-ups.

Notice the Apostle makes it very clear that Jesus is not in my soulish nature, my brain. But wherever He is living, He is living in me by faith. Now this has to help me, comfort me, and strengthen my security in Him.

My faith must work apart, far apart, from my soulish nature. It works in and flows out of my heart, my spirit nature, the inner man; and from this source, my faith operates.

Romans 10:9 speaks about my mouth confessing, but it is with the heart that I believe. Paul said to the jailer, *Believe on the Lord Jesus Christ, and thou shalt be saved* (Acts 16:32). The jailer did receive. He confessed, and it all felt so good, especially while Paul was with him.

So many would like to maintain those first glorious days of soulish delight. We soon learn, however, that faith does not function by feeling. We discover what Paul was talking about in Romans 8—the battle with the flesh, that carnal, fleshly mind I call the brain. In verse 11, there is a quickening that is supposed to take place in us because of God's Holy Spirit indwelling the believer.

Volumes have been written on the book of Romans. Study it over and over again. Know its great truth, but be ready until the day you die to deal with your own flesh, with the brain as its agent, seeking ever to discourage you.

Is it possible for us to find a way to offset the force of the flesh, to offset the imagination of the brain, to really and truly live out the crucifixion Jesus experienced for us?

The Lord spoke to me one day and said, "Teach My people that they cannot out think the Devil." What He was suggesting is that we can lose the war of the brain versus the mind of Christ if we don't know how to do battle.

I replied to Him how that made sense to me because Satan was smarter and more experienced than we were.

When I asked what we could do, He answered me, "You can out talk him."

When I asked why that could be, He replied, ''Because Satan couldn't answer me back.'' Of course, all of us know that we win all one-sided conversations.

Since Satan can only work through our thought processes, our wonderful Lord is trying to help us overcome this source of so much of our frustration. The brain (our carnal thoughts—past, present, and future) can only be overcome by a verbal use of the tongue. Only with powerful words of faith and Scripture can we successfully battle the greatest source of our insecurities.

The tongue will speak out either for the flesh or for the heart. If we use our tongue to give aid and comfort to the flesh, then the heart—that which we believe with, the God-given spirit within us that knows the Creator can do all things—is neutralized, offset, nullified, and voided.

If, in our brain, we receive doubts, fears, and unbelief which we have carried over from childhood, and then continue to practice them, speak them, and live them, we are truly carnal Christians, weak and sickly, remaining very insecure.

This chapter could be a book in itself because the Bible so vividly portrays the battle which saints have with their fleshly mind.

The story of David and Bathsheba is a good example of a great man falling because he gave in to his carnal brain. As a shepherd boy, his was a believing mind. He experienced what God could do by the victories he received over the bear and the lion. Young David was the only person in Israel who was ready to face Goliath, the giant.

That which caused David, the giant killer, to fall has caused many of God's choicest men to fall. They did not know how to combat the temptation that came to their flesh by what they saw and heard.

What should David have done when he saw Bathsheba bathing, especially when he learned she was another man's wife? He should have averted his eyes, then sung the Twenty-third Psalm and worshiped God. Just by using his tongue to speak Scripture, David could have caused the temptation that was so demanding at the moment to pass.

David had many beautiful wives that God had given to him to satisfy his desires. Many a twentieth-century David has fallen, who also had a beautiful wife. He suffers disgrace; his church suffers, and his family suffers. This happens all too frequently.

There is an answer to Satan's temptation in the fleshly brain. It is to use the mind of Christ, a set *will* that speaks out loud and says, as Jesus said, "Not My will, but Thine be done." The words of the mouth, spoken out of the depth of the heart (the mind of Christ), will offset the evil that appeals to the fleshly brain.

Childhood insecurities, if allowed to go unchallenged, will always interfere with the Lord's security that wants to flow from our hearts where He dwells and through our mouths, bypassing our carnal brains, to build up the new mind of the Spirit.

I have overcome many of my childhood insecurities by doing this, by simply confessing Christ as the Source and strength of my life. These tricks of the enemy and the carnal brain are thus offset, and I am free to become what He wants me to be.

A Prayer

Dear Father, I am so glad You laid all my sins and evil thoughts on Your Son, Jesus. He took all my sins and gave me complete pardon, so that I will never have to meet them in heaven.

Thank You for helping me to allow the new mind of Christ—the mind that loves God and hates evil—to grow big inside me.

Thank You that I know now how to deal with this carnal brain. I will set my new mind of the spirit to serve You, and with my mouth I will continually confess Your greatness and my love to You.

In Jesus' name,
Amen.

7
Inability To Forgive

For if ye forgive men their trespasses, your heavenly Father will also forgive you: but if ye forgive not men their trespasses, neither will your Father forgive your trespasses.

Matthew 6:14,15

Then came Peter to him, and said, Lord, how oft shall my brother sin against me, and I forgive him? Till seven times?

Jesus said unto him, I say not unto thee, Until seven times: but, Until seventy times seven.

Matthew 18:21,22

And his lord was wroth, and delivered him to the tormentors, till he should pay all that was due unto him. So likewise shall my heavenly Father do also unto you, if ye from your hearts forgive not every one his brother their trespasses.

Matthew 18:34,35

Judge not, and ye shall not be judged: condemn not, and ye shall not be condemned: forgive, and ye shall be forgiven.

Luke 6:37

Then said Jesus, Father, forgive them; for they know not what they do.

Luke 23:34

Our Lord Jesus had much to say about forgiveness. As they say in some circles today, "He blew their mind!" Peter, the Lord's disciple, thought if he could forgive someone seven times, he would be making a great impression on the Lord. But Jesus answered in such a way that Peter knew he wasn't even close to understanding this key word *forgiveness.*

Is *forgiveness* really a momentous and significant word? Is Jesus merely talking about a small spiritual challenge, or is He talking to us about one of the "biggies" in our life?

The Scriptures plainly teach us that unless we are constantly forgiving, there is no forgiveness coming from our Father to cover our own sins.

Even if we can firmly establish that forgiveness is a key spiritual word, how can we connect it with what this book is all about: security versus insecurity?

Who will have the easiest time of forgiving: a secure person or an insecure person?

Who will carry grudges the longest: one who is secure or one who is insecure?

Who is quick to forgive, quick to make up, the first to go to another when there is ought to forgive?

I believe we can all agree that the secure Christian will have the least difficulty with these important matters.

Insecurity begins at an early age because its symptoms result from both hereditary and environmental causes. Thus, it becomes a fixed part of life and very difficult to face or even acknowledge, much less do away with. Because there are so many broken homes, with people carrying heavy grudges and filled with bitterness, it is even more troublesome today than it was before.

What causes people to carry this grudge? They carry it because they are unwilling or unable to forgive the offense, or because it has been driven deep into their subconscious mind.

Before dealing with how to become a secure and forgiving person, let us talk about the problems that will result if we do not. Besides the awesome, unthinkable spiritual results, we have the resulting physical sicknesses plaguing the unforgiving.

Medical science teaches that most sicknesses (up to 90 percent) are caused or brought about through psychosomatic emotions (wrong thinking, fears, pressures, hatred). Unforgiveness heads the list of these psychosomatic emotions.

Here are some illustrations I know about, having been personally involved either with the story or with the healing.

One of our pastors was robbed by another Christian of many thousands of dollars. He didn't realize how hazardous or damaging his unforgiveness was until his hands began to swell with arthritis. Being a young man in his thirties, this was shocking. He went to the Lord with the problem and, as a result, truly forgave the person. In a very few hours, his arthritis was gone.

I have known of Christians who had suffered from migraine headaches for over twenty years and, in spite of prayer, there was no healing forthcoming until forgiveness was expressed. Then the headaches vanished.

Another situation of unforgiveness caused continuous prayers for another to go unanswered until forgiveness was extended. Then the answer to prayer was forthcoming.

By my personal knowledge, the following problems have resulted because of an unforgiving heart: years of painful, physical suffering from migraines, arthritis, rheumatism, even surgery; unanswered prayer; marital difficulty and divorce. I could go on and on. The list would grow if all results could be tabulated.

How do we receive help for the insecurity resulting from such unforgiveness? For our answer, let us look to the most secure Person ever to live on the face of the earth.

Jesus Christ had for His father not an earthly one, but a heavenly One. He did not inherit in His genes a fallen race, plagued by all its resulting weakness. He had to be the most secure Person ever to live among men.

Even by the farthest stretch of your imagination, you can't see Him hating someone, carrying a grudge, gossiping, backbiting, being resentful or even competitive. He treated all people alike. He played no favorites. He was not defensive, did not defend, was not jealous, did not lash out in anger. He was so secure that He fell asleep during a raging storm at sea.

How could He look down from the cross and say, *Father, forgive them*? He could because He had the kind of security that looked ahead.

Looking unto Jesus the author and finisher of our faith; who for the joy that was set before him endured the cross, despising

*the shame, and is set down at the right hand
of the throne of God.*

Hebrews 12:2

Jesus saw more than hypocritical Pharisees and Roman soldiers with spears. He saw Himself, far ahead, sitting joyfully with His Father in glory.

A secure, forgiving person cannot be looking back, reliving the pains and rejections of the past. He must look ahead, anticipating the joys of being forgiven. This can only happen as forgiveness is extended to others.

Some of the best advice I have ever heard for those who have difficulty forgiving others is to pray for them. Pray that they will be saved, be healed, be blessed. As you pray for them, forgiveness is much easier.

Much of what causes insecurity early in life stems from experiences with others: abuse, rejection, dis-appointment, frustrations, even ridicule. These *past* experiences, if not faced, will continue to be *daily* experiences. Forgiveness is not just a once-in-a-while thing; it must be a way of life. It is a life-style that will be a happy, secure one.

A Prayer

Dear Lord Jesus, I come to You for help because You were so forgiving when You experienced the abuse of men. Please help me to extend toward others that same spirit of forgiveness.

You commanded me to forgive. You would not have commanded me to do this if You had not made me secure enough to do so. I believe I have that security.

Now, in Your name and in Your power, I forgive everyone their trespasses against me. I know I have Your forgiveness because I have forgiven.

Thank You, Lord.
Amen.

8
Self-Centeredness

Two men went up into the temple to pray; the one a Pharisee, and the other a publican.

The Pharisee stood and prayed thus with himself, God, I thank thee, that I am not as other men are, extortioners, unjust, adulterers, or even as this publican. I fast twice in the week, I give tithes of all that I possess.

And the publican, standing afar off, would not lift up so much as his eyes unto heaven, but smote upon his breast, saying, God be merciful to me a sinner.

I tell you (Jesus is saying), this man went down to his house justified rather than the other: for every one that exalteth himself shall be abased; and he that humbleth himself shall be exalted.

Luke 18:10-14

Self-centeredness (or narcissism) begins very early in life. Perhaps it is the first negative childhood characteristic that surfaces.

Friends come to visit you, bringing their child into your home. Your child watches as the young visitor makes a beeline for his toy box. The fight and tug of war over the toy, often observed, speaks loudly of a weakness of insecurity that surfaces and seems to follow us doggedly the rest of our lives.

Self-centeredness surfaces in many ways: pride, selfishness, covetousness, self-exaltation, ostentatiousness, self-justification. It can be loud talk, dominating the conversation; raucous laughter, drowning out all others; or outlandish, peculiar clothing.

Self-centeredness also will be displayed by comparing ourselves with other people to make ourselves look better. Usually a very poor loser gloats much over victory. Many times compliments are canceled out by the voice of someone else pointing out a weakness.

Jesus' parable of contrast between the Pharisee and the publican is a good, descriptive comparison for us to ponder. It is a large mirror into which we should all take a long hard look. As we do, I believe we will see much childhood insecurity following us, even into our Christian life, that contributes much to our immaturity. This is not an image we should walk away from and promptly forget, as the Apostle James suggests we are usually doing.

Jesus said that the Pharisee stood and prayed with himself. This self-centered, selfish prayer is an apt description of well over 90 percent of all prayers. "Lord, bless me, and my family—us four and no more" is a little rhyme that is all too familiar. The Pharisee thinks only of himself. He thinks he is much better than anyone else.

How can a self-centered person do otherwise? How can he ever get to know someone else, their families, their problems, and their needs? He is wrapped up in only one person: himself. This began, no doubt, in his childhood; and as an adult, he has yet to face it and begin to prayerfully acknowledge it before the Father.

Notice that, in the Pharisee's prayer, he contrasts himself with the sins of others which he thinks are worse. How many times have you heard someone say, "I am not any worse than most people I know, and probably a little better," or "If I go to hell, all my friends will be there with me." Yes, and even those who know God can remain self-centered if they refuse to face this insecurity.

The world of the insecure, self-centered person is a small one. Even his religious life, including church fellowship, is small.

As a supervisor of many churches, I have watched this religious insecurity and self-centeredness surface when a new pastor in a church begins to draw in new people. When the saints, who have been in that church, sitting in the same pew every Sunday and seeing the same faces, are suddenly forced to sit somewhere else, shake hands, and—horror of horrors—even be hugged by a visitor, their little religious vacuum is shattered.

Of course, they have said "Amen" to the pastor's prayer each Sunday—the prayer that was lifted up to God on behalf of the city and neighborhood for sinners to be saved. But being so narcissistic (or self-centered) and insecure, they couldn't have meant that "Amen." As God answered their prayer, new people began to come in and force a change in their religious environment. Apparently they became unhappy that God had answered their prayer.

It is possible that these deep, unchallenged insecurities in the saints were the culprit that has caused the dismissal of pastors and the red light that has stopped the fresh breath of revival. In many instances they have even caused a church split.

Jesus, in talking about loving our neighbors as we do ourselves, was endeavoring to break us out of this deadly mold. It is painfully apparent that the Pharisee had not been able to do this, or couldn't do it, as he looked around for someone with which to compare himself, to make himself look better.

The commandment to love your neighbor as yourself will cause you to think of others first. We all love ourselves sufficiently already. We, no doubt, began at that point as children. Now we must make the painful, obedient switch.

The neighbors and their needs must become the ones you remember first as you lead your family in prayer.

The government and those in authority should be the first ones we corporately remember (2 Tim. 2:1,2) as we pray together at the church service, reaching out and away from ''us four and no more.''

Let us come closer to home as we remember Paul's words to the Ephesians:

So ought men to love their wives as their own bodies. He that loveth his wife loveth himself.

Ephesians 5:28

The remedy for many marital problems rests with the husband. Paul has already commanded the wives to submit to their husbands in the same manner they submit to the Lord. (Eph. 5:22.) If the wife is submitting—and the Word of God requires her to do so—then the complete responsibility rests on the man.

The husband is the head of the wife the same as Christ is the head of the Church. He is to love her as he loves himself. When he endeavors to do this, he will find himself fighting against all of his childhood insecurities. From a child, if not taught differently (and most of us were not), he was turned inwardly: "*My* toy, *my* daddy, *my* mother, *my* house." As an adult, he must turn and put somebody else first: his wife, his children, his church, and of course his Lord.

Because men have not been taught to face this insecurity, they are deeply frustrated in their marriage relationship. Divorce is on every hand in the Christian home, as well as in the world. This ought not be; not just the broken home and the divorce, but the frustration and conflict in the Christian life that so many seem to experience.

We must face the insecurities that plague us. How do we find help after we have knowledge of the weakness of self-centeredness, self-consciousness, and selfishness?

Jesus has the answer for us as He contrasted the two men in prayer. The Pharisee prayed from selfish pride; the publican prayed from deep humility and in acknowledgment of his sins. We must face our earthly, apparent weakness as saints, inasmuch as the righteousness of Christ has taken care of our eternal righteousness. As we face these earthly insecurities, our wonderful Lord will help us. He wants to and He will.

We can overcome our weaknesses by taking them to Him. Let us face our selfishness in our marriages. Most of us love ourselves more than we love each other. Through repentance, we are to acknowledge this. It is not a better husband or wife that we need but a bigger heart. Divorce doesn't solve problems, it creates them.

The publican prayer, *Be merciful to me*, caused him to be justified. God heard that prayer and He will hear yours. Not only was His mercy and grace available for the time we prayed as sinners, it is constantly available as we live this Christian life. God, our loving Father, wants to meet all our needs as we look to Him to help us and heal us from our insecurities.

A Prayer

Dear Father, I acknowledge the insecurities that have followed me into my Christian life. They hinder me from loving my neighbor as myself and my wife (or husband) as I love my own body.

Dear Lord, I want to be a big person, free from this weakness of self-centeredness. I want to be a godly neighbor and a good husband (or wife) and parent.

By Your help, I will put others' needs first. I will stop talking about myself and putting others down. I will become a good listener. I will humble myself before You and, with Your help, will stop being self-centered.

I ask this, Father . . .

in Jesus' name,
Amen.

9
Criticism

Nearly everything and everybody gets berated at some time. This holdover from childhood learning, caused by a critical spirit, heads the list of security robbers.

From earliest childhood people have heard someone or something being criticized. It started with the weather: "It's going to be another hot one!" or "Looks like rain again . . . when will it ever stop?" or "I'll be glad when winter is over!"

As a result of hearing all this, they grew up saying the same things. Even the weather forecaster was criticized. Some kids probably grew up thinking he caused the weather, rather than just predicting it.

Then, of course, there were the neighbors. They always got a tongue-lashing. They were criticized for the color of paint they put on their house, the kind of car they drove, the way they dressed, how they raised their kids, how they lived their married lives . . . on and on, ad infinitum!

Whatever the conversation was, you can rest assured that someone was being criticized. Oh, and don't forget the politicians! In a Republican household, the Democrats were criticized. In a Democratic household, the Republicans were criticized. Some probably thought God was a Republican and the Devil was a Democrat, or vice versa.

Many people grew up in such a negative, critical home. From the first time they went to school, their eyes viewed the world through critical lenses. They criticized the way other kids dressed, the way the teacher dressed, the kind of lunch that was served in the school cafeteria. They were experts on how people should talk, walk, dress, and live. After all, *their* parents, grandparents, brothers, and sisters were right; and anyone who differed was wrong.

Then they started going to church. It was the thing to do because they had heard that all those who didn't attend were terrible.

After church, they had the preacher for dinner—only he wasn't there! His sermon, his wife, his family, the car he drove—all came up for critical scrutiny. It was hard for children to understand. Hadn't they heard their parents tell him at the door how much they had enjoyed his sermon?

By the time dinner was over, they had critiqued, not only the preacher, but everyone else at church that morning.

The time came for children of church-going families to confess their faith in God. If you grew up in such a home, when you were old enough, you received the sacraments, baptism, and church membership. You did it very sincerely. You did love the Lord and believe in Him, and there was an awakening in your heart.

You began to learn about His righteousness and the security you had in your faith, but why didn't you grow spiritually as you should? Looking back on it now, what hindered your growth? Why was it that your belief in Jesus and the Word, and your participation in the worship, did not cause you to grow spiritually mature? Some will never know.

May I candidly suggest that the maturity and security of Christ did not develop because you had already developed, in hard concrete, some very bad habits that stopped your spiritual growth.

Our insecurity is alarmingly evident because of childhood habits that continually surface to plague us. Thus, we are preventing the security of Christ from becoming a vital part of our lives.

Listen as the Lord speaks to you from Psalm 15:1-3:

Lord, who shall abide in thy tabernacle? Who shall dwell in thy holy hill?

He that walketh uprightly, and worketh righteousness, and speaketh the truth in his heart.

*He that **backbiteth not** with his tongue, nor doeth evil to his neighbour, nor taketh up a reproach against his neighbour.*

"You are forever talking against your brother, stabbing your own mother's son in the back."

Psalm 50:20 NEB

"You do this [backbiting] and expect me to say nothing? Do you really think I am like you?"

Psalm 50:21 (paraphrased)

In Romans 1:30, backbiters are mentioned along with haters of God. James 2:1-9 expresses condemnation to those of us who allow these childhood habits to continue to be a part of our life-style. They will not keep us out of heaven, but they will hinder the security of our Lord from developing maturity in our Christian life-style. Notice verse 10:

For whosoever shall keep the whole law, and yet offend in one point, he is guilty of all.

Knox says he "is liable to all its penalties."

Just being aware of this negative inheritance of criticism that had become an uncorrected habit has allowed more of His security to begin to surface in my life as I work to curtail this treacherous hang-up.

Remember Paul's words to the Romans: *Let us not therefore judge one another any more* (Rom. 14:13).

Do not allow this chapter and its admonition to become a legalistic noose that will choke your developing Christlike life-style. As you stop criticizing, His security will be allowed to flow, and you will enjoy a healthy body and a solid spiritual relationship with Him. He is Lord.

A critical nature is the opposite of a complimentary one. While there will always be something in all of us to criticize, there is also something to compliment. (Some great person once said there is so much bad in the best of us and so much good in the worst of us that it does not behoove any of us to talk about the rest of us.)

Why do we continually put people down and make them feel inferior? If one person brags on another, we have a habit of thinking hard to recall something negative we have heard about that person.

Controlling the tongue, even though it might have a legitimate gripe, is a must. Listen with your heart as you read James 1:26:

If any man among you seem to be religious, and bridleth not his tongue, but deceiveth his own heart, this man's religion is vain.

Here is a good paraphrase: Anyone who puts forth much effort with his heart trying to please God, while at the same time makes no effort to control his tongue, will waste his effort to please God. Not only that, but everything he hoped to receive will not happen because he is constantly deceiving, contradicting, voiding out, setting aside, and rendering useless his heart—the inner part of him that believes in God.

The tongue—that little member which is set on fire of hell—must be controlled. It will stop the flow of the security of the believer. It will nullify all maturity before the heart can be enriched by the Word of God. All efforts to grow will be stymied.

The next time you start to criticize someone, **stop** and think of something good to say.

But I say unto you, That every idle word that men shall speak, they shall give account thereof in the day of judgment.

For by thy words thou shalt be justified, and by thy words thou shalt be condemned.
Matthew 12:36,37

A Prayer

Dear Father, I desire, above everything else, a life that is free from a critical spirit. I desire to become that person who walks in pleasing ways in Your sight.

Please help me to overcome the negative attitudes I acquired while growing up in a sinful society. I want to love people as You do, to see the best in them, and to stop my tongue from pointing out their weaknesses.

Inasmuch as You received me, a worthless sinner, just as I was with all my faults, help me to be like-minded toward others.

In Jesus' name,
Amen.

10
Inability To Take Correction

A wise son heareth his father's instruction: but a scorner heareth not rebuke.

Proverbs 13:1

For the commandment is a lamp; and the law is light; and reproofs of instruction are the way of life.

Proverbs 6:23

Whoso loveth instruction loveth knowledge: but he that hateth reproof is brutish [stupid].

Proverbs 12:1

"And he who hates reproof will die [physically, morally and spiritually]."

Proverbs 15:10 AMP

For whom the Lord loveth he correcteth; even as a father the son in whom he delighteth.

Proverbs 3:12

All scripture is given by inspiration of God, and is profitable for doctrine, for reproof, for correction, for instruction in righteousness.

2 Timothy 3:16

We have all been acquainted with people who are reluctant to receive instruction or correction. They would rather try it and be wrong than ask advice. When advice is offered, they turn it down. Proverbs 12:1 says it so well, calling such an attitude "stupid."

Why will a person refuse help, going through life turning a deaf ear to it? Is it possible that this, too, is because of deep-seated insecurity?

Perhaps it can also be traced back to our original parents when they refused God's instruction. Many believe that if

Eve had asked Adam about eating of the fruit before she ate, we would not be in this sinful state today.

Children, to begin with, are very insecure in many ways. If you hand them a new toy and try to show them how it works, they will usually pull away, and only come back for instruction when they give up trying their futile way. All of us have heard the familiar saying, "You do it your way; I'll do it mine," not fully realizing that insecurity could be showing.

This childhood insecurity develops more strongly in some than others. But all of us have a measure of it following us into adulthood, even into our new life as Christians. As long as we refuse to acknowledge this inherited trait, we keep the security and maturity of our Lord from developing within us.

This trait is very noticeable in college students. I have observed this in many of them as it is my privilege to teach in several colleges. The young student will usually listen from a highly critical viewpoint. It would be wonderful if all of us could go through life first, *then* go to college to learn—*after* we have become secure enough to listen objectively.

Though Israel saw with their own eyes the great miracles of our Lord, their insecurity would not allow them to change. This type of insecurity, if allowed to go unchecked, will end with a stubborn, unteachable spirit.

For rebellion is as the sin of witchcraft, and stubbornness is as iniquity and idolatry.
2 Samuel 15:23

If your family, neighbors, or friends have a way of doing something that is better, why not give it a try? If a brother or sister in the faith seems to be making more progress than you, would it not be a good idea to at least inquire as to why this is so? Maybe they can help you. This will put you into a much better position or posture than later feeling threatened by their apparent success.

The type of insecurity that leads to an unteachable spirit has gone undetected in the average Christian church. The majority of believers in the faith will remain in the church affiliation of their parents. Very seldom are they open even to discuss other faiths. Yet they readily admit that they do not practice the teaching they know is contained in the Word of God; and that when they read scriptural truths they are not experiencing, they are troubled.

If a person is secure in what he believes, surely he would be open to discuss the Word of God without being defensive. Many will develop a "blind spot" in their spiritual perception because of this. Even the Apostle Paul would not be welcome in their church if he taught all that he wrote to the New Testament churches.

Perhaps it is this same spirit of insecurity that causes some to be so vastly different from others. We witness this in dress, in color preference, in style of living. Very often it becomes evident in older people. Being insecure within their age bracket, they seek to lower their age in the eyes of others by dressing and acting much younger than they are.

Parents especially are the ones I hope to help with this book. They will not only realize *their* insecurities, but will be able to detect these early symptoms in their children and give instruction so that they will develop into secure young people.

A good example of things to avoid can be learned from parents who lived during the depression of the thirties. These parents keep reminding their children of how terrible it was. In doing so, they pass on a fear to their children. I am sure I have been guilty of this many times, having lived during that trying era.

Being secure enough as a person and as a Christian will always cause you to be open to correction and instruction. If you find yourself resenting others when they try to help you, remember that it can be a result of your childhood insecurity following you into adulthood.

As a born-again believer, you are a very secure person in Christ. If you know who you are and where you are going, you are far ahead of your unsaved friends. But because we do not recognize these symptoms of insecurity and deal with them, the life of the Lord Jesus cannot surface in us.

Note these powerful verses:

. . . nor receiveth correction: truth is perished (Jer. 7:28).

They have refused to receive correction: they have made their faces harder than a rock (Jer. 5:3). (See also Prov. 29:17; Job 5:17; Prov. 13:24.)

These are only a few of the many scriptures which teach us the intrinsic value of correction. If a person is not open to receive correction, the truth will perish. A corrected son is a happy, secure son, who will bring delight to his father's heart. He that hates reproof or resents correction is a dying person.

God corrects or chastens those whom He loves. To put it another way, He corrects those who have an ongoing relationship with Him. Many Christians cannot receive correction from God because of a poor relationship with their own fathers.

This current charismatic renewal has, along with the many rich blessings of the Lord that have accompanied it, surfaced many insecurities in His people. Some of our leading pastors have publicly resisted what God is doing today.

A secure pastor, who believes in his own relationship with Jesus, will not resist what God is doing. He will allow God to do what He wants to do and will simply say, ''I am in God's will, conducting my church services according to His will. I am very happy for my brother who is doing differently and is being blessed.''

A secure denominational Christian will not refuse to receive the ''new thing'' or better life in the spirit. He wants to be open to correction, not closed to it and thus, perchance, miss out on one of the world's greatest revivals.

I have one hobby: golf—one of the most difficult of games in the sporting world to conquer. It always amuses me to see a beginner, or even one who has golfed for a long time, refuse to receive instruction or correction. Though he needs the help, he will not ask for it and, even worse, he resents anyone who might offer to give a tip. Why is that? One reason: because of his insecurity.

A secure person, no matter how well he is doing, is always open to suggestions in order to better himself.

Most parents know that their children seem to be born with much insecurity. They will resist any help, even in how to play with a new toy. Only when they have failed to operate it will they ask for help.

Some people's insecurity will surface in their refusal to receive correction due to their obesity. They say, "I have tried everything! I don't want to hear about it anymore!"

The answer to our childhood insecurity, that which follows us into our adult Christian life, is the Word of God. The Scriptures are given to us for correction. We need to constantly read them, listen as they are taught, and give heed to them—to be doers of the Word and not hearers only.

The hard heart will not receive instruction. A secure person has a very soft heart and is eager to be helped.

I have noticed in my confrontation with the cultists who go from door to door that most of them—at least those with whom I have dealt—are highly insecure people. They could fit most of the chapter headings in this book. They are highly defensive, always putting others down, and won't admit error. They will not listen and are very impatient to be on their way to the next door, as though their security consists in how many calls they make.

A secure Christian who knows the Word of God will listen, ask good questions without flaring up in anger, and not feel threatened. He is secure in his facts.

Another way this kind of insecurity surfaces is in a person who is always correcting someone else. A certain amount of help or instruction is usually appreciated, but to be constantly harassed by another's opinion is very aggravating. The person who gives so much instruction and correction is usually not overly open to it himself.

If the Word of God is indwelling you as a believer, you are in an ever-learning posture before your Lord and before your peers.

Ye are of God, little children, and have overcome them: because greater is he that is in you, than he that is in the world.

1 John 4:4

With the knowledge that the Greater One is in you, you will be able to deal with the insecurities which have plagued you from childhood.

Confess constantly that He is in you. Confess *His* strength, not *yours*. Confess *His* indwelling ability, not *your* ability. Do not speak of all the things you do not have or cannot do. Speak only of who you are in Him.

Your cords of security will grow stronger and stronger as your insecurity disappears.

A good Christian is characterized by true humility. A humble spirit is a teachable one, and a teachable one can be found only in a Christian who is endeavoring to correct the insecurities that constantly plague and harass him.

Arm yourself with the scriptural fact that the Greater One indwells you as a child of God, even greater than all hindrances and hang-ups. Once armed, use that armor by constantly confessing who you are in Christ, not who you are by natural birth. God is your new Parent. You now have the same Father as your Lord had. Speak openly of His security.

A Prayer

My wonderful Father, Who loves me so very much, please forgive me for allowing the weakness of the fallen nature to continue to hinder my walk with You. Help me to face these Adamic weaknesses of the first Adam and take on the strength of the new Adam.

By Your help, I refuse to be stubborn or unteachable. I open my heart to Your correction and will obey Your commands. I will not resent those who endeavor to help me.

I humble myself at Your feet and desire to be one of Your very own secure children.

In Jesus' name,
Amen.

Conclusion

Security in Christ is fertile soil in which faith can grow. Insecurity, often beginning in childhood and continuing into adult life, breeds unbelief.

Jesus talked about the devastating results of our idle words; that is, words we speak carelessly or thoughtlessly. Many times these non-working, idle words are a result of our being brought up in a very insecure society.

The following are some examples of idle words, sentences that we need to strike from our vocabulary if we want to become more secure and productive:

"I can hardly believe that!"

"That's hard to believe!"

"That can't be true!"

"That's impossible!"

"That's incredible!"

This kind of statement, spoken without thought, can cause our heart to think it is extremely difficult to be a believing heart—especially to believe what God can do! If we are having difficulty believing something we have heard, it would be far better to say, "All things are possible with Him," or "God is able."

With the response of, "That's hard to believe," we tend to further harden our hearts toward the exercising of our faith. Why not say, "With God all things are possible." Then we would be exercising our hearts and mouths toward faith's possibility.

Another expression we need to drop is, "Well, if it is going to happen to anyone, it will happen to me!" Let us analyze this statement with an illustration.

The church service is over and we are walking toward our cars. As you approach yours, several people call attention to the fact that your vehicle has a flat tire. If you responded with the above negative statement, then I would answer, "Do you mean to say that if anything bad is going to happen, it would happen to you? That if anyone were slated to get cancer, it would be you?"

You would no doubt say, "Oh no, I didn't mean that!"

Don't you see? You are teaching your heart to disbelieve the words your mouth is speaking. Then, sometime in the future when you have a desperate need and your heart *must* believe the words of God (*rhema*) which you are saying, you will be in trouble because you have taught your heart to ignore the words of your mouth.

The words and cliches we learned in a godless and insecure society must be changed to conform with our new-found security in Christ Jesus our Lord. Thus we are teaching our hearts to believe the words of our mouths.

A Prayer

Dear Father, please forgive me for uttering idle words, words that taught my heart to ignore the power of my speech. I want my heart to believe all of the finished work of the Cross.

Help me to use my tongue to speak only those words with which my heart can agree. I know, by Your help, I can become that secure person who is truly secure in Christ my Lord.

In Jesus' name,
Amen.

References

The Amplified Bible. Published by Zondervan Publishing House, Grand Rapids, Michigan. Used by permission.

The Holy Bible, The Berkeley Version in Modern English. Gerrit Verkuyl. Published by Zondervan Publishing House, Grand Rapids, Michigan. Used by permission.

The New English Bible. Published by Collins World, © Oxford and Cambridge University Presses, Great Britain. Used by permission.

The New Testament in the Language of Today. William F. Beck. Published by Concordia Publishing House, St. Louis, Missouri. Used by permission.

The New Testament in the Translation of Monsignor Ronald Knox. Published by Sheed and Ward, Inc. and Burns and Oates, Ltd., New York. Used by permission.

Roy H. Hicks is a successful minister of the Gospel who has given his life to pastoring and pioneering churches throughout the United States. He has served the Lord in various foreign  fields, having made missionary journeys to South America, the Orient, Australia, and New Zealand.

As a dedicated man of God, Dr. Hicks serves today as General Supervisor of the Foursquare Gospel Churches and has become a popular speaker at charismatic conferences.

Perhaps the things that most endear Dr. Hicks to readers is his warmth and his ability to reach out as the true believer he is—a man of strong, positive faith, sharing a refreshing ministry through the power and anointing of the Holy Spirit.

To contact Dr. Hicks, write:
Dr. Roy H. Hicks
Foursquare International Headquarters
1100 Glendale Boulevard
Los Angeles, California 90026